Small Blessings

Hope & Encouragement from

Our Daily Bread

Compiled by Dave Branon

Our Daily Bread Publishing™

Design by Mark Veldheer

An Our Daily Bread Ministries Exclusive Edition

Printed in the United Kingdom

22 23 24 25 26 27 28 / 7 6 5 4 3 2 1

Introduction

The idea for this book came because of the kindness of an *Our Daily Bread* reader.

A few years ago, I received a package from that reader. When I opened it, I was pleasantly surprised to find a plaque with a saying on it; people do send me things like this from time to time. Upon closer inspection, though, I was further surprised to discover that the saying was something I had written for *Our Daily Bread*. Because a particular sentence had special meaning to the reader, she copied it on some nice parchment-type paper and mounted it on a wooden frame.

When I first saw that memento from a thoughtful reader, it sparked an idea. For a long time after that, I toyed with the idea of compiling a book of sayings from the pages of the devotional guide we've been producing at Our Daily Bread Ministries since 1956. When I became an editor at Discovery House (now Our Daily Bread Publishing) in 2008, I had the opportunity to pursue this idea. I began gathering poignant or helpful or thought-provoking lines written over the past few years by *Our Daily Bread* writers.

What I found was a treasure trove of pithy sayings that can benefit us all. As I gleaned more and more of these maxims from the pages of *Our Daily Bread*, I realized their value. After all, each of us can use little reminders from time to time to trust God more or to refresh our fellowship with Him or to be newly awed by His greatness. We all need those occasional, gentle nudges that remind us to pray more diligently or witness more courageously or give more generously.

The process of picking these thoughts from *Our Daily Bread* also reinforced the reality of the richness and depth of the Bible. As you look through the pages of *Small Blessings*, you'll notice that each adage is accompanied by a passage of Scripture. Indeed, each adage is not just accompanied by the Bible verse—it is actually built upon that biblical truth. The words we as writers compile for *Our Daily Bread*, no matter how well they might be arranged, would have no meaning whatsoever if they were not predicated on and in adherence with the truths of God's inspired Book. They are not presented as representative of man's wisdom but instead are attempts to present God's teachings in a fresh way that is memorable and meaningful. The goal of each writer is to share the richness and depth of the life-changing wisdom of the Bible.

Our desire in presenting this compilation to you is to encourage you. In a world of frightening changes and sometimes foreboding events, it's good to be able to immerse ourselves in the majesty of God's goodness and the hopefulness of His truth. The nature of this book allows you to savor one teaching or several, depending on what you need each day. But each time you pick up this book, we hope you will feel invigorated and encouraged spiritually—as my *Our Daily Bread*–reader friend was when she read the quote she made into a plaque.

Oh, in case you are curious, you can discover what that little plaque said by going to the last saying in this book. She titled that plaque "Starting Today," which is a great way to describe the challenge of living for Jesus in an invigorating, new way.

Dave Branon
Compiler

How we live our lives today as followers of Christ is our "note" to the world.

BILL CROWDER

You do not know what will happen tomorrow. For what is your life? It is even a vapor that appears for a little time and then vanishes away.

JAMES 4:14

Any resolution to follow God is not a casual promise.

MARVIN WILLIAMS

Leave your gift there before the altar, and go your way. First be reconciled to your brother, and then come and offer your gift.

MATTHEW 5:24

Our lives are not made by the dreams we dream but by the choices we make.

JOE STOWELL

And this I pray, that your love may abound still more and more in knowledge and all discernment, that you may approve the things that are excellent.

PHILIPPIANS 1:9–10

The traits today's children need to guide a future society do not come by accident, but through diligent, godly parenting.

DAVE BRANON

Behold, children are a heritage from the LORD, the fruit of the womb is a reward.

PSALM 127:3

Christlike kindness can open the door for a heart-touching testimony.

VERNON GROUNDS

Imitate me, just as I also imitate Christ.

1 CORINTHIANS 11:1

ON
OFF

No matter what kind of voice you have, when you sing the words of Scripture back to God, it is sweet music to His ears.

CINDY HESS KASPER

Let the word of Christ dwell in you richly ... in psalms and hymns and spiritual songs, singing with grace in your hearts to the Lord.

COLOSSIANS 3:16

It takes grace to give godly correction; it takes greater grace to receive it.

DAVID ROPER

Faithful are the wounds of a friend.

PROVERBS 27:6

In times of struggle and despair, it is helpful to recall that we are pilgrims traveling between the eternities.

BILL CROWDER

These all died in faith, not having received the promises, but having seen them afar off were assured of them.

HEBREWS 11:13

Who needs you to be God's arms of love today?

DAVE BRANON

Let us not love in word or in tongue,
but in deed and in truth.

1 JOHN 3:18

Welcoming God's Word to penetrate the deep, dark places of our hearts is the only way to find true healing and the spiritual health we long for.

JOE STOWELL

The word of God is living and powerful,
. . . a discerner of the thoughts and
intents of the heart.

HEBREWS 4:12

If we judge others only by their outer appearance, we might miss the wonderful surprise of what's in their heart.

BILL CROWDER

The LORD does not see as man sees;
for man looks at the outward appearance,
but the LORD looks at the heart.

1 SAMUEL 16:7

Heartache has a way of pointing us to the Lord Jesus, who has shared in our sufferings and can bring meaning to seemingly senseless pain.

DENNIS FISHER

It was necessary for the Christ to suffer and to rise from the dead the third day.

LUKE 24:46

The Lord can chisel His image on our flawed lives and make us beautiful.

ALBERT LEE

Choose for yourselves this day whom you will serve . . . But as for me and my house, we will serve the LORD.

JOSHUA 24:15

Expose the darkness by living in the light.

ANNE CETAS

It is shameful even to speak of those things which are done by them in secret.

EPHESIANS 5:12

The important thing is being remembered not by others, but by God.

JULIE ACKERMAN LINK

Remember me when You come into Your kingdom.

LUKE 23:42

Keep a wide gulf between yourself and your possessions.

HERB VANDER LUGT

It is hard for a rich man to enter the kingdom of heaven.

MATTHEW 19:23

The forces of sin outside cannot defeat the life of Christ inside.

JULIE ACKERMAN LINK

Now abide faith, hope, love, these three;
but the greatest of these is love.

1 CORINTHIANS 13:13

God graciously offers us forgiveness for what is past and wisdom for what yet lies ahead.

MART DEHAAN

Can a man take fire to his bosom, and his clothes not be burned?

PROVERBS 6:27

In a world where words are often wielded as weapons, may we use our words as tools to build up the hearts of others.

BILL CROWDER

A man has joy by the answer of his mouth, and a word spoken in due season, how good it is!

PROVERBS 15:23

Instead of focusing on what is wrong, let's obey the One who knows what is right.

JULIE ACKERMAN LINK

Cease to do evil, learn to do good;
seek justice, rebuke the oppressor.

ISAIAH 1:16–17

The next time you stumble, remember that the powerful hand of God is holding your hand and walking you through life—all the way home.

JOE STOWELL

Nevertheless I am continually with You;
You hold me by my right hand.

PSALM 73:23

Even in life's toughest circumstances, we can, with God's help, enjoy a measure of healing.

DAVE BRANON

This is my comfort in my affliction,
for Your word has given me life.

PSALM 119:50

The One who created this universe out of nothing has a history of accomplishing the impossible.

C. P. HIA

With God all things are possible.

MATTHEW 19:26

To glorify God means that we have the high privilege of showing Him off in a world that is totally unaware of what He is really like.

JOE STOWELL

Therefore, whether you eat or drink, or whatever you do, do all to the glory of God.

1 CORINTHIANS 10:31

The hard times we endure are God's way of preparing us for greater service for His glory.

CINDY HESS KASPER

[We are] heirs of God and joint heirs with Christ, if indeed we suffer with Him, that we may also be glorified together.

ROMANS 8:17

No church will be a perfect fit, but we can all work at fitting together more perfectly.

JULIE ACKERMAN LINK

[Christ], in whom the whole building, being fitted together, grows into a holy temple in the Lord.

EPHESIANS 2:21

When we belong to the King of kings, we need no other bragging rights!

JOE STOWELL

He chose us in Him before the foundation of the world, that we should be holy and without blame before Him in love.

EPHESIANS 1:4

God's love is a rushing stream that flows from His heart into ours.

DAVID MCCASLAND

We love Him because He first loved us.

1 JOHN 4:19

True strength comes when we stop trying to control people and start serving them instead.

JULIE ACKERMAN LINK

Whoever desires to become great among you, let him be your servant.

MATTHEW 20:26

We are just one prayer away from connecting with the God of the universe.

DAVE BRANON

Whatever you ask in My name, that I will do, that the Father may be glorified in the Son.

JOHN 14:13

God's approval is always sweeter than the applause of the crowd.

CINDY HESS KASPER

We make it our aim . . . to be well pleasing to Him.

2 CORINTHIANS 5:9

Allow God to spread the fragrance of His love through you today.

ANNE CETAS

If God so loved us, we also ought to love one another.

1 JOHN 4:11

The next time fear creeps into your life, don't panic. God can be trusted in the darkness.

JENNIFER BENSON SCHULDT

Whenever I am afraid, I will trust in [God].

PSALM 56:3

Authentic love is a gift from God that we can keep on giving.

DAVID ROPER

Love never fails.

1 CORINTHIANS 13:8

The important thing with the work we do is that God likes what He sees.

DAVE BRANON

Be steadfast, immovable, always abounding in the work of the Lord, knowing that your labor is not in vain in the Lord.

1 CORINTHIANS 15:58

Christmas proves that God keeps His promises.

JOE STOWELL

She will bring forth a Son, and you shall call His name Jesus, for He will save His people from their sins.

MATTHEW 1:21

If only perfect people qualified to serve God, He wouldn't have anyone to choose from!

JOE STOWELL

You are inexcusable, O man, whoever you are who judge, for in whatever you judge another you condemn yourself; for you who judge practice the same things.

ROMANS 2:1

When we trust God's goodness, we are fed by His faithfulness.

JULIE ACKERMAN LINK

Trust in the LORD, and do good; dwell in the land, and feed on His faithfulness.

PSALM 37:3

True freedom comes when we allow Christ to rule our hearts.

DAVID MCCASLAND

Sanctify the Lord God in your hearts.

1 PETER 3:15

Our cares cannot compete with God's Word.

JENNIFER BENSON SCHULDT

I rise before the dawning of the morning, and cry for help; I hope in Your word.

PSALM 119:147

The key to going the distance is the discipline of running every day.

DAVID MCCASLAND

Run in such a way that you may obtain [the prize].

1 CORINTHIANS 9:24

Calling sin by a softer name will change neither its offensiveness to God nor its cost to us.

C. P. HIA

How can I do this great wickedness, and sin against God?

GENESIS 39:9

The Bible doesn't keep us from enjoying life; it makes true enjoyment possible.

JULIE ACKERMAN LINK

Turn away my eyes from looking at worthless things, and revive me in Your way.

PSALM 119:37

What have you done today that will last for eternity?

JOE STOWELL

Where your treasure is, there your heart will be also.

LUKE 12:34

Worship doesn't involve behaving as if nothing is wrong; it's making sure everything is right—right with God and with one another.

JULIE ACKERMAN LINK

Then Mary took a pound of very costly oil of spikenard, anointed the feet of Jesus, and wiped His feet with her hair.

JOHN 12:3

Life, love, and chocolate taste better when shared with others.

CINDY HESS KASPER

Be imitators of God . . . . And walk in love, as Christ also has loved us and given Himself for us.

EPHESIANS 5:1–2

True wealth is not measured by what you have but by who you are in Christ.

JOE STOWELL

I counsel you to buy from Me [Jesus] gold refined in the fire, that you may be rich.

REVELATION 3:18

Praise God that even when we don't understand Him, we know we can trust Him.

DAVE BRANON

I am God, and there is no other; I am God, and there is none like Me.

ISAIAH 46:9

To please the Lord, we must do His work His way.

ALBERT LEE

The fear of the LORD is a fountain of life,
to turn one away from the snares of death.

PROVERBS 14:27

Diminish your distractions by making Jesus your focus.

MARVIN WILLIAMS

Martha was distracted with much serving.

LUKE 10:40

A life well-lived is directly related to a Bible well-read.

DAVID MCCASLAND

Open my eyes, that I may see
wondrous things from Your law.

PSALM 119:18

Strong faith and a good conscience make a winning combination.

HERB VANDER LUGT

Having faith and a good conscience, which some having rejected, concerning the faith have suffered shipwreck.

1 TIMOTHY 1:19

Resentment fades when the object of our ill will becomes the object of our goodwill.

DENNIS DEHAAN

You shall not . . . bear any grudge against the children of your people, but you shall love your neighbor as yourself.

LEVITICUS 19:18

For the Christian, death is not a dark journey into the unknown; it is a glorious transition into the joys of heaven.

RICHARD DEHAAN

We are confident, yes, well pleased rather to be absent from the body and to be present with the Lord.

2 CORINTHIANS 5:8

Praise is our enthusiastic response of gratitude to God.

JULIE ACKERMAN LINK

Praise the LORD!

PSALM 150:1

We can rest in the truth that God is in control.

ANNE CETAS

Shall the one who contends with the Almighty correct Him?

JOB 40:2

God makes miracles out of what seems insignificant: fragile faith, a little kindness, and ordinary people.

JULIE ACKERMAN LINK

Your daughter-in-law, who loves you, . . .
is better to you than seven sons.

RUTH 4:15

Our union with Christ makes us saints, but our obedience to God's Word through the power of the Holy Spirit makes us saintly.

MARVIN WILLIAMS

To the saints and faithful brethren in Christ who are in Colosse.

COLOSSIANS 1:2

Faith is trusting God's goodness in spite of life's troubles.

DAVE BRANON

Everyone who asks receives, and he who seeks finds, and to him who knocks it will be opened.

LUKE 11:10

Although money is not evil, it can prevent us from inheriting true riches if accumulating it is the goal of our lives.

JULIE ACKERMAN LINK

The genuineness of your faith [is] more precious than gold.

1 PETER 1:7

When we aim our lives at God's Word, we'll discover that His ways are right on target—every time!

JOE STOWELL

Teach me Your way, O LORD;
I will walk in Your truth.

PSALM 86:11

As God's Word spreads from our heads to our hearts, sin loses its power over us.

JULIE ACKERMAN LINK

Your word I have hidden in my heart,
that I might not sin against You.

PSALM 119:11

The evidence of God's salvation can be seen in our faces, heard in our voices, and reflected by the works of our hands.

DAVID MCCASLAND

Oh, sing to the LORD a new song!
For He has done marvelous things.

PSALM 98:1

The closer we get to God, the more like Him we will become.

DAVID ROPER

LORD, who may abide in Your tabernacle?
Who may dwell in Your holy hill?
He who walks uprightly.

PSALM 15:1–2

Deep relationships are built on acceptance, understanding, and listening.

HERB VANDER LUGT

Oh, that you would be silent,
and it would be your wisdom!

JOB 13:5

If you feel as if you are drifting off course, there's no better time than now to heed God's voice and return to the fold.

DAVID MCCASLAND

All Scripture is given by inspiration of God, and is profitable for doctrine, for reproof, for correction, for instruction in righteousness.

2 TIMOTHY 3:16

The only fitting response to God's grace is to serve Him in humility and love.

HADDON ROBINSON

But I have trusted in Your mercy;
My heart shall rejoice in Your salvation.

PSALM 13:5

When looking at others makes you resent the unfairness of life, change your focus. Look to Jesus.

HERB VANDER LUGT

Jesus said to him, "If I will that he remain till I come, what is that to you? You follow Me."

JOHN 21:22

As God's people, we must love the truth, look for the truth, and live by the truth.

DAVE BRANON

As you therefore have received Christ Jesus the Lord, so walk in Him, rooted and built up in Him and established in the faith.

COLOSSIANS 2:6–7

We must banish prejudice and unfair attitudes from the inner citadel of our hearts.

DENNIS DEHAAN

No one calls for justice,
nor does any plead for truth.

ISAIAH 59:4

Trusting in the sovereignty of God can turn outrage into compassion and hatred into concern.

HADDON ROBINSON

Do not be overcome by evil,
but overcome evil with good.

ROMANS 12:21

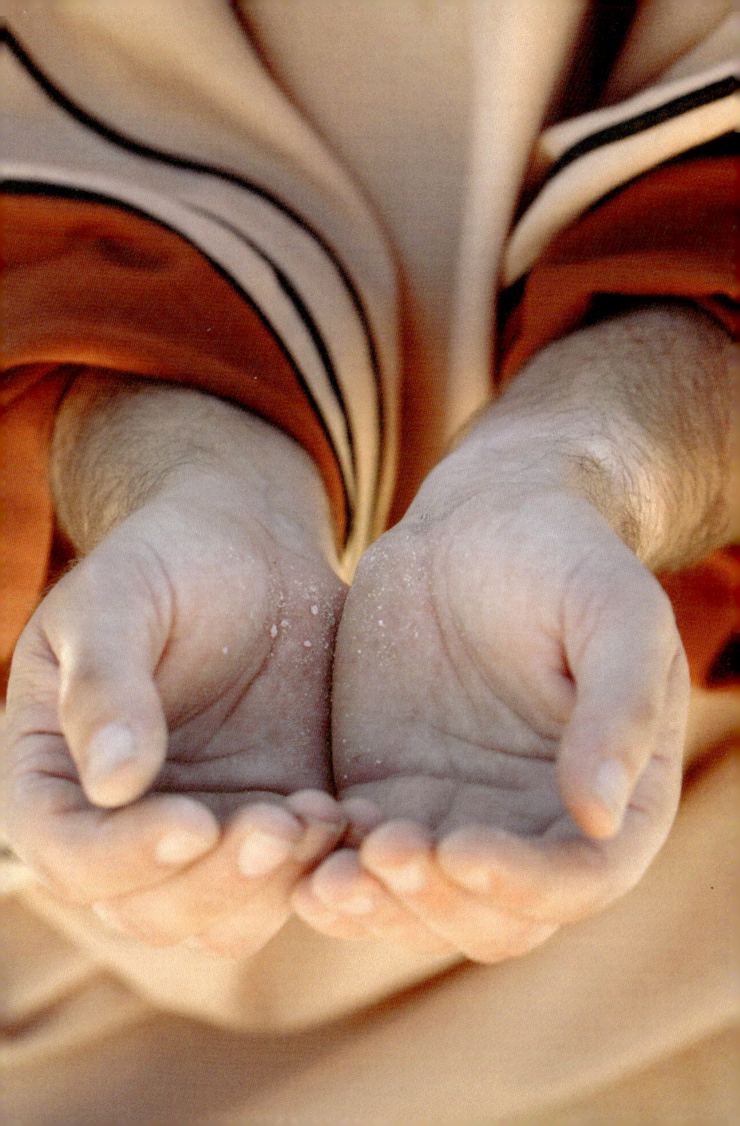

A sharp tongue leaves a scar, while a helpful word heals the heart.

DAVID MCCASLAND

There is one who speaks like the piercings of a sword, but the tongue of the wise promotes health.

PROVERBS 12:18

Treat a critic as a friend, and you both win.

DAVE EGNER

The way of a fool is right in his own eyes,
but he who heeds counsel is wise.

PROVERBS 12:15

Let's take care that we don't express our opinions as if they were God's words.

MART DEHAAN

Do not add to His words, lest He rebuke you, and you be found a liar.

PROVERBS 30:6

Courage is not the absence of fear but the mastery of it.

DAVID ROPER

[Jesus] said to them, "It is I; do not be afraid."

JOHN 6:20

Cherish the gift of life, and savor the joy of God's handiwork.

DAVE BRANON

I will praise You, for I am fearfully
and wonderfully made.

PSALM 139:14

The wonderful life God offers is found only in radical obedience to His commands.

MARVIN WILLIAMS

From that time many of His disciples went back and walked with Him no more.

JOHN 6:66

Instead of jumping into a situation with the presumption that God is on our side, we need to be certain that we are on His.

JULIE ACKERMAN LINK

The LORD searches all hearts and understands all the intent of the thoughts.

1 CHRONICLES 28:9

Significance is not found in the number of our days, but in what our eternal God says about how we have used them.

MART DEHAAN

Fear God and keep His commandments, for this is man's all.

ECCLESIASTES 12:13

Reading the Bible thoughtfully turns our minds into storehouses through which the Spirit can work.

RANDY KILGORE

My word . . . shall not return to Me void, but it shall accomplish what I please.

ISAIAH 55:11

Wherever we are and whatever we're doing, God wants to be a part of it.

DENNIS FISHER

Pray without ceasing.

1 THESSALONIANS 5:17

If you are enduring a great trial of affliction, remember this: For this you have Jesus!

HENRY BOSCH

For He Himself has said, "I will never leave you nor forsake you."

HEBREWS 13:5

The church is healthy only when we work together, look out for each other, and use our strengths to benefit one another.

JULIE ACKERMAN LINK

There should be no schism in the body, but . . . the members should have the same care for one another.

1 CORINTHIANS 12:25

True success is staying on God's path by following His Word and giving Him praise.

DAVID MCCASLAND

When you were little in your own eyes,
. . . did not the LORD anoint you king
over Israel?

1 SAMUEL 15:17

It's never too late to start building on the Rock.

DAVID MCCASLAND

Whoever hears these sayings of Mine, and does them, I will liken him to a wise man who built his house on the rock.

MATTHEW 7:24

Learning to benefit from failure is the key to continued growth in grace.

DENNIS DEHAAN

If anyone sins, we have an Advocate with the Father, Jesus Christ the righteous.

1 JOHN 2:1

When we trust ourselves to God's keeping, we are forever secure.

VERNON GROUNDS

You, O LORD, shall endure forever,
and the remembrance of Your name
to all generations.

PSALM 102:12

When we submit our goals and desires to the Lord, we can be sure that He will give us what is best.

DAVE BRANON

The Son of Man did not come to be served, but to serve, and to give His life a ransom for many.

MARK 10:45

Ask God today to give you a newness of spirit, a freshness of faith, and a renewed appreciation of His love.

CINDY HESS KASPER

Restore to me the joy of Your salvation.

PSALM 51:12

The Holy Spirit keeps us honest, focused, and encouraged so we can glorify Christ.

DAVID MCCASLAND

When He, the Spirit of truth, has come,
He will guide you into all truth.

JOHN 16:13

God is relentless in His love for us—ever-pursuing, ever-present, and ever-guiding.

DAVID ROPER

Where can I go from Your Spirit?
Or where can I flee from Your presence?

PSALM 139:7

STAY ON PATH

When we submit our plans to God's will, we can enjoy His peace in the midst of life's uncertainty.

VERNON GROUNDS

You do not know what will happen tomorrow.

JAMES 4:14

Hope, peace, and a zest for living—they all spring from being in love with Jesus.

DAVID MCCASLAND

For God so loved the world that He gave His only begotten Son, that whoever believes in Him should not perish but have everlasting life.

JOHN 3:16

Prayer is placing ourselves in the presence of God to receive from Him what we really need.

DAVID MCCASLAND

Your Father knows the things you have need of before you ask Him.

MATTHEW 6:8

Christ bought us—body, soul, and spirit. Let's make sure we let Him use the total package for His glory.

DAVE BRANON

You were bought at a price; therefore glorify God in your body and in your spirit, which are God's.

1 CORINTHIANS 6:20

Rather than looking everywhere for breathtaking moments, we should find meaning in every breath we take.

JULIE ACKERMAN LINK

A man has nothing better under the sun
than to eat, drink, and be merry;
for this will remain with him in his
labor all the days of his life.

ECCLESIASTES 8:15

As each day unfolds, we must pause and remind ourselves that this is a day dedicated to God, that it is to be used for His glory, and that it is best lived with a continual recollection of what Jesus did for us on the cross.

DAVE BRANON

[Jesus] said to them all, "If anyone desires to come after Me, let him deny himself, and take up his cross daily, and follow Me."

LUKE 9:23

Our Daily Bread® Writers

The date indicates the writer's first appearance in *Our Daily Bread*. An asterisk notes that the writer is still an active contributor.

Henry Bosch April 1956

Dave Branon April 1989*

Anne Cetas September 2004*

Bill Crowder June 2006*

Dennis DeHaan January 1996

Mart DeHaan January 1973*

Richard DeHaan April 1956

Dave Egner January 1982

Dennis Fisher May 2005

Vernon Grounds September 1993

C. P. Hia April 2008*

Cindy Hess Kasper October 2006*

Randy Kilgore January 2011

Albert Lee October 2002

Julie Ackerman Link December 2000

David McCasland May 1996

Haddon Robinson January 1993

David Roper December 2000

Jennifer Benson Schuldt September 2010*

Joe Stowell February 2007

Herb Vander Lugt July 1967

Marvin Williams February 2007*

Joanie Yoder September 1994

Scripture Index

Help us get the word out!

Our Daily Bread Publishing exists to feed the soul with the Word of God.

If you appreciated this book, please let others know.

- Pick up another copy to give as a gift.
- Share a link to the book or mention it on social media.
- Write a review on your blog, on a bookseller's website, or at our own site (odb.org/store).
- Recommend this book for your church, book club, or small group.

Connect with us:

@ourdailybread

@ourdailybread

@ourdailybread

Our Daily Bread Publishing
PO Box 3566
Grand Rapids, Michigan 49501 USA

books@odb.org